THE DISPLACED OF CAPITAL

PHOENIX **POETS**

THE
DISPLACED OF
CAPITAL

ANNE WINTERS

THE UNIVERSITY OF CHICAGO PRESS
Chicago and London

ANNE WINTERS is associate professor of English at the
University of Illinois at Chicago. She is the translator of
Salamander: Selected Poems of Robert Marteau, and the author
of a book of poems, *The Key to the City*, published by the
University of Chicago Press.

The University of Chicago Press, Chicago 60637
The University of Chicago Press, Ltd., London
© 2004 by The University of Chicago
All rights reserved. Published 2004
Printed in the United States of America

13 12 11 10 09 08 07 06 05 04   1 2 3 4 5

ISBN: 0-226-90233-1 (cloth)
ISBN: 0-226-90235-8 (paper)

Library of Congress Cataloging-in-Publication Data

Winters, Anne.
    The displaced of capital / Anne Winters.
        p.   cm.—(Phoenix poets)
    ISBN 0-226-90233-1 (cloth : alk. paper)
    ISBN 0-226-90235-8 (pbk. : alk. paper)
    1. New York (N.Y.)—Poetry. 2. Social problems—Poetry.
3. Homelessness—Poetry. 4. Poverty—Poetry.
I. Title II. Series.

PS3573. I539D57 2004
813'.54—dc22   2004004210

♾ The paper used in this publication meets the minimum
requirements of the American National Standard for
Information Sciences—Permanence of Paper for Printed
Library Materials, ANSI Z39.48-1992.

This book is for my daughter
Elizabeth

Contents

Acknowledgments

Grateful acknowledgment is made to the editors of publications in which the following poems first appeared:

At Length: "An Immigrant Woman"
Chicago Review: "Cold-Water Flats"
The New Yorker: "Wall and Pine: The Rain"
Paris Review: "The First Verse"; "Villanelle"
Slate: "Old Law Flats"; "*Tosca* with Man in Bedrock"
Storie (Rome): "The Brown Owl of Ulm"
Tikkun: "The Displaced of Capital"
Triquarterly: "Three Images"; "The Mill-Race"; "The Grass Grower"

I. THE MILL-RACE

The Mill-Race

Four-fifty. The palings of Trinity Church
Burying Ground, a few inches above the earth,
are sunk in green light. The low stones
like pale books knocked sideways. The bus so close to the curb
that brush-drops of ebony paint stand out wetly, the sunlight
seethes with vibrations, the sidewalks
on Whitehall shudder with subterranean tremors. Overhead, faint flickers

crackle down the window-paths: limpid telegraphy of the
late afternoon July thunderstorm unfurling over Manhattan.
Its set and luminous velocity, long stalks of stormlight, and then the first drops
strike their light civic stripes on the pavement.
Between the palings, oat-panicles sift a few bright
grains to the stonecourse. Above it, at shoulder height
a side door is flung open, fire-exits; streaming from lobbies

come girls and women, white girls in shadowy-striped rayon skirts, plastic
    ear-hoops,
black girls in gauzy-toned nylons, ripples of cornrows and plaits,
one girl with shocked-back ash hair, lightened eyebrows;
one face from Easter Island, mauve and granitic;
thigh on thigh, waist by waist; the elbow's curlicue and the fingers'; elbow-
    work, heel-work,
are suddenly absorbed in the corduroyed black rubber stairs of the bus. Humid
sighs, settlings, each face tilts up to the windows'
shadowless yards of mercuric green plate glass. An

interspace then, like the slowing of some rural
water-mill, a creaking and dipping pause
of black-splintered paddles, the irregularly
dappled off-lighting—bottle-green—the lucid slim sluice
falling back in a stream from the plank edge. It won't take us
altogether, we say, the mill-race—it won't churn us up altogether. We'll keep
a glib stretch of leisure water, like our self's self—to reflect the sky.
But we won't (says the bus rider now to herself). Nothing's
left over, really, from labor. They've taken it all for the mill-race.

In close-ups now, you can see it in every face,
despite the roped rain light pouring down the bus-windows—
it's the strain of gravity itself, of life hours cut off and offered
to the voice that says "Give me this day your
life, that is LABOR, and I'll give you back
one day, then another. For mine are the terms."
It's gravity, spilling in capillaries, cheek-tissue trembling,
despite the make-up, the monograms, the mass-market designer scarves,

the army of signs disowning the workplace and longing for night . . .
But even as the rain slackens, labor
lengthens itself along Broadway. The night signs
come on, that wit has set up to draw money: O'DONNELL'S,
BEIRUT CAFE, YONAH'S KNISH . . . People dart out from awnings.
The old man at the kiosk starts his late shift, whipping off rainstreaked
lucite sheets from his stacks of late-market newsprint.

If there is leisure, bus-riders, it's not for you,
not between here and uptown or here and the Bronx.
Outside Marine Midland, the black sea of unmarked corporate hire-cars
waits for the belated office lights, the long rainy run to the exurbs;
and perhaps on a converted barn roof in Connecticut
leisure may silver the shingles, somewhere the densely packed

labor-mines that run a half mile down from the sky
to the Battery rise, metamorphic, in water-gardens,
lichened windows where the lamp lights Thucydides or Gibbon.

It's not a water-mill really, labor. It's like the nocturnal
paper-mill pulverizing, crushing each fiber of rag into atoms,
or the workhouse tread-mill, smooth-lipped, that wore down a London of
    doxies and sharps,
or the flour-mill, faërique, that raised the cathedrals and wore out hosts of dust-
    demons,
but it's mostly the miller's curse-gift, forgotten of God yet still grinding, the salt-
mill, that makes the sea, salt.

The Grass Grower

I
In 1979, a woman who lived in West Harlem took a snapshot
of a man who grew grass in the courtyard, her father-in-law.
In a summer hat, the thin face acute, serene . . . As on the first day

I glimpsed his counter and sign, JOEL HARMON, RADIO REPAIRS,
   propped in
or part of the pawnshop's mixed economy, so those last evenings
you seemed to be simply conducting, in silence, your life.

—My brow pressed to the shop-pane, the shade of the cast iron balls
and Amsterdam's carhorns, a dog somewhere snapping and whining—
inside, arms angled strangely, you were prising

a cathedral radio's cabinet from its mounting. It was 1949.
I was in the sixth grade, and slow to go home. I'd drift through the shop
you kept alone at that hour, or climb on a stool and listen; for we

talked a lot, in that early time, or you did. Flipping knobs, half-effacing
your cool inflections with QXR or local Harlem
"race-music" . . . Shawville, a town west of Selma, you named

as a birthplace, and Georgia, where you were married.
"Alabama's no place for the black man" (you said) "but a Jim Crow town
in North Georgia is hurtful to man, displeasing to God."

Line by line you gave me Jim's portrait, his subtle subsets. "Say you're
colored, got to go downtown out of your own part—make sure
you don't drink water, and think through your memory-map

where you're going— 'Here I can hand in prescriptions, but stay
standing up.' Or 'There I can sit: Jim-Crowed to the end of the counter.'
There's no signs, like some think up here—you work it yourself." You ignored

our own strange suchness (seemed to), skinny white kid, black vet with pale
burn-bubbles on his forearms. You preferred history—told me how slaving
   marched almost
as many to death as Hitler, Stalin—liked words

that bit into things, anecdotes, numbers
because they stood free from your voice, that even you
must have sometimes wished to escape. One bad story

gave me your wife's name, a story from Georgia. "It must
have been on our marriage-date. For her present, we'd picked
a hat-store downtown, supposed to sell to our color. But 'Stay out,'

the store lady said to me—like a dog. Said to stay out. But I could see Sue
asking to try on a hat; first they dropped a square of cotton
cloth on her head, then sort of dropped the hat

on top—no way my wife's going to finger-tip-touch that hat—and she looked,
cloth in one eye, such a *fool*— Well, those were my thoughts,
you know, at that moment . . ." When I showed, even past trying to show,

my shock at the cloth, you stopped me (it was like you): "That's state law;
she sells some colored-touched hat to white folks, she goes to jail . . ."
In fact, coming back to the *why* of your talking, was it

for transmission? Already I sensed your assignment: to order your past,
live your life as history, number—to name the effectual powers.
"When they called me up, I found out Jim ran the army . . ." Like my father,

you'd no word for combat for me, but one day coming in—you were on the
    phone,
back turned—I heard the long syllables I that came back years later
cycling north of the Seine through the hay-ricks and spires of Amien, Rouen . . .

Of course I could see through your shirt your ribbed, olive-drab
undershirt, twin to my father's—why, he'd done boot-camp
in Georgia, I'd *lived* there. But I never saw

that, not being my father, you couldn't know that, or that I could speak up
and tell you. So I'd sensed, by then, that Jim, and not you, was the subject;
my father had never met Jim. But I liked transmission, it was something

I could be there for. And so, for years as it seemed, I heard you tell
how, on the boat back, after a poker game, you made the resolve
not to go below Mason-Dixon again—"COLORED FOR SWEEP-UP ONLY—
    And I kept it,

Jim made me a grass-widow man here in Harlem. I wasn't about
to go South again after . . . the Army, and Sue . . . So I never raised
my own kids. But how could I go back, you tell me. Just tell me that thing."

II

I had something else on my mind, in the late fifties and sixties,
than you. I was scared—of my childhood, of Harlem, your own
aridity; your all-too-imaginable ironies, too, on my sporadic

Civil-Rights doings. So I can't guess what you felt, when the events you'd
    schooled
your life toward took on their dates and place names. It seems eerie, today, as
    Harlem
outsoars Bangladesh in early deaths, rediscovers TB—that the year I met you
    again

in Walgreens, and our late visits began, it might have seemed Jim
would someday slip from the world . . . Your son, his wife June, had moved to
    New York.
She often dropped in; you'd a super's apartment just off Columbus,

and had gone all quiet. I'd sit and watch you boil water in a skillet
("It's faster") for coffee, on your pre-war range, your profile against a seedy
screen frayed thin at the perimeter . . . A few words about your grandson, or

the grass-growing. A sugar bowl full of seed, a trowel, the nightly
waterings . . . It was strange. "Where do you get the grass-seed?" (Politely.)
Your far-off smile (you wore glasses, now): "I get it from the grass."

As if, your histories fallen away, each practice of the present
brimmed up in you silently—when June came, you lifted the kitchen chairs
into the court "to enjoy the evening." But she, who was pregnant again,
    preferred

to walk up and down, while you cooled the concrete before her
with hose-spray. You'd fountained its cracks and random fissures
with grass-tufts, untrimmed, fantastic, running to seed . . .

I tilted my chair back. Night had fallen. Your glasses were dim octagonals
in the arc-light that fell through the cyclone fencing. Past two buildings that lay
in rubble (the long slide had begun), in the next block, we could glimpse

the high glare of downtown, a few outscaled towers, and, nearer,
the gray lights of stacked stairwell windows. From the far side
of your nature, no word arrived . . . Only the night watering

went on, sparkling tracings as you came forward, your back
to the streetlamp, your freshets waist-high in the darkness, thumb-misting
the tips of the grasses with idle tendrils of light.

The Displaced of Capital

"A shift in the structure of experience . . ."
As I pass down Broadway this misty late-winter morning,
the city is ever alluring, but thousands of miles to the south
the subsistence farms of chickens, yams and guava
are bought by transnationals, burst into miles
of export tobacco and coffee; and now it seems the farmer
has left behind his ploughed-under village for an illegal
partitioned attic in the outer boroughs. Perhaps
he's the hand that emerged with your change
from behind the glossies at the corner kiosk;
the displaced of capital have come to the capital.

The displaced of capital have come to the capital,
but sunlight steams the lingerie-shop windows, the coffee bar
has its door wedged open, and all I ask of the world
this morning is to pass down my avenue, find
a fresh-printed *Times* and an outside table;
and because I'm here in New York the paper tells me of here:
of the Nicaraguans, the shortage of journeyman-jobs, the ethnic
streetcorner job-markets where men wait all day but more likely the women
find work, in the new hotels or in the needle trades,
a shift in the structure of experience.

A shift in structure of experience
told the farmer on his Andean plateau
"Your way of life is obsolescent." —But hasn't it always been so?

I inquire as my column spills from page one
to MONEY&BUSINESS. But no, it says here the displaced
stream now to tarpaper *favelas*, planetary barracks
with steep rents for paperless migrants, so that they
remit less to those obsolescent, starving
relatives on the *altiplano*, pushed up to ever thinner air and soil;
unnoticed, the narrative has altered.

Unnoticed, the narrative has altered,
but though the city's thus indecipherably orchestrated
by the evil empire, down to the very molecules in my brain
as I think I'm thinking, can I escape morning happiness,
or not savor our fabled "texture" of foreign
and native poverties? (A boy tied into greengrocer's apron,
unplaceable accent, brings out my coffee.) But, *no*, it says here
the old country's "de-developing" due to its mountainous
debt to the First World—that's Broadway, my cafe
and my table, so how can I today
warm myself at the sad heartening narrative of immigration?
Unnoticed, the narrative has altered,
the displaced of capital have come to the capital.

An Immigrant Woman

PART ONE

I

Slip-pilings on the Brooklyn littoral
—the poles still tarry, flimsy; the ferry terminus
with its walledup doors wan doorshapes
on eroded sills. Downstream, the strutwork
of the Williamsburg cable tower
threw its cool shadow half a mile inland
over tarpaper seams, gantried water butts,
and splintery tenement cornices milled
with acanthus and classical grasses
of nineteenth-century dream-slum fantasy.
We could see, from our rooftops, the endspan
floating its ant-threads of traffic
to the granite salients of the anchorage,
and through its strands on the west
the Financial District's watery silhouettes.

But it was our own foundations, crumbling
in the sandy soil, that made us protest
the drill rigs sounding for a wider bridge ramp

to funnel the airport traffic over us
into Manhattan. "Construction tremors
will weaken our buildings": from the over-roosted
tenements clinging near the anchorage
flew manuscript lists of signatures, block-groups'
painfully Englished petitions. But City Hall
adoze, sleep-feeding, just flooded us

II

with chimerical figures and blueprints,
wearing us down. Our own "block-leader," Luz,
a Guatemalan law student at NYU
where I studied classics, distracted us
more easily with her "pure language"
or anti-Puerto Rican tirades. "Call that Spanish?
Take my sitter—*muy indio*, still speaks some
Maya mountain-language BUT
the beautiful Spanish!" And so one evening this sitter,
Pilar, came over—forty, perhaps, with a long
fawn-tinted oval face, and read in low tones
an archaic poem to the Madonna. "My daughter
knows it in Quiché and English—" and she passed around,
wistfully, a First Communion photo—flat cheekbones
like her mother's, long black braids, straight look.

Luz told us Pilar had lost husband
and son to the *Violence*; a machine-gunned
death heap in the center of their village—
"They killed all the men. But when my family
came here, she came with her girl, we helped with the
green card, and she's a hotel maid now
near the UN . . ." Much realer, this, than our own
bridge-inflicted, some-day disaster. And who knew
but our bridge might metamorphose,
as the City said ("Global cities draw capital"), into a river
of money ("We'll all sell *cuchifritos* on the ramp"),
and anyway, mainly, summer

was running out, with its open evenings
and windows. One Saturday, turning onto my block
from the subway, I heard my name, crossed
the street where twin buildings had area-ways.
and saw you waving, the same, Pilar,
from a window below the swag-bellied area railings.
"Come have some coffee—go around in back."
I walked down the building-side, and turned in a trash-littered
airwell by a door with multiple doorbells.
You opened from a wooden hallway, unpainted,
with padlocked doors. "See, the super's cut up his flat
for illegals. They took out an inside wall, so our room
has a window—we all share the bath." I entered
a lime-walled room—chairs and table, sofa-bed. Your front wall
was the building front, the three others
drywall. On the bureau, a black-shawled
prie-dieu: two photos; two candles in translucent, white-waxed sacks,
and a polychrome Madonna with meeting brows.

Through your window, car wheels, railings; and, above,
my own second-story windows. "We saw you
reading there," you said from behind me, "when we moved in."
You sat me on the sofa, and formally presented your daughter
(she moved her schoolbooks all to one end.) Near her, a shallow,
linoleumed-over trench and a bathroom sink. You said:
"I'm a widow from the mountains near Morache, very near
the home-town of Señora Luz. My real work is hotel maid, and I've got
a nice job, at a place called the Tricontinental."
Then you paused, and I felt how clearly
you'd presented yourself, as Americans do, with your job,
your *état civil*, and I said: "I'm a graduate student

at NYU, where Luz studies, no, not married, no children . . ."
I tried to add something else at once, to leave this less . . .
definitive, but nothing came, so we ran through bridge-rumors,
and soon we were hardly listening, waiting
for our own next word, and laughing at our gabble. Pequita
told us what the priest had said
about the drilling; you spoke of Pequita's
First Communion, and none of us could stop
finding striking things to say. Next day you came over
to see my plants, and I came back for soup-supper, looking up
at my windows, which in the easy half-yellow light
of autumn looked oddly beckoning. As we ate,
you leaned forward, with a sudden rogue's smile,
and mockingly proposed that we three walk across the bridge,
"There's a path up there. If the bridge
is bad, we'll tell off the Mayor—" (In what spirit, I wondered,
had you listened to our committee?) And when I got home
I looked down, and through your sheer curtains saw you
cleaning up, and Pequita, at the table, reading.

But next week, instead of the plank stair
that zigzags up the anchorage-side, we wandered
the riverside shipping alleys. From below, we could see
overhead the under-arch of the bridge, and feel
the resonant top-thrum of westbound
subways and trucks. Then the riverside—I loved
this part. A sort of post-industrial fenworld, with tiny
terrace houses, big dredger-parts laid aside
from the drillings, and abandoned wreckers' lots
filled with sea-floor light and trembling, long-awned
panicles of switchgrass. Its timelessness
soothed me—though ephemeral. Even that day, one freshly
tuckpointed facade, and a pair of brandnew bronze
Edwardian mermaid doorknockers. I could see
our quarter five years from now, say—the withering
discount chains, tentative boutiques,
and mother and daughter figuring, to the upscale
"pioneers," as neighborhood indigenes, living on
with strange literalness among them, supplying
their just-permissible quantum of urban grit.

You were ahead, and Pequita trailed us, rattling weed stalks
with a stray lath. As we progressed in and out
of the endspan's slatted shadows, you turned
and called me into a side-lot—sunken concrete, flask-
green puddles, to a broken-off building wall. It had been
interior, once—rows of soiled roomsized
plaster squares trailing sawn pipes, with one high trembling
toilet, like a pearl. In a lower square, fringed
with ailanthus and barbs of gang graffiti,
was a mural. *Muy latino*: the mountain

dreaming the city: a terrace cafe with palm trees
and a dancer shawled in black lace, with inward-angled
castanets. And you lifted yourself on tiptoe,
Pilar, to touch the lace, as you might have grazed
Pequita's cheek. I felt a pang, as if I already needed you
sturdy inside your sturdy body, not this gesture
as if, exiled within, you reached out— We stepped
back, museum-wise, to contemplate, and you said:
"Luz likes to say I'm some mountain-woman, but when
my mother died, I lived with my aunt in the City—I only
went back when I married." I told her I'd lived
in this city, with a stepmother, who'd divorced my uncle
to marry my father; and beat me. "A stepmother's
a curse of God," you said gently. And on the walk back,
pointed out more wall palms, beaches, until New York
seemed a dot in a belt of capitals
high on the globe: world-cities, packed
with immigrants, refugees, *Gastarbeiter:* a snowy
latitude suffused with tropical nostalgia.

V

We were a threesome. Coffee, suppers, TV,
Pequita at my computer—you'd asked me to teach her—
or sleeping on my sofa, one bad month
they moved you to night shift. Yet only that summer,
I'd worked in my window like a scholar
in a lamplit bay, the night filled with myriad noises,
like Roman Juvenal, to whose ears "came ever
the sounds of buildings collapsing." Across, the two
tenement-faces, florid, all bucrania, meanders, dusky trails
of fire-escape bedding. And everything underlit
by the sinister, slow-stopping car lights of our street.

But now it was the dailiness of two
from another hemisphere. Through snow-fissures, winds fluting
on railings and building-flaws, Pilar in her low frame
paced with armfuls of laundry, washed
in the sink and hung to dry everywhere. The thousand
stratagems of those who simply *must not* spend;
and the tiny mother-decisions: though you preferred
periphery, housekeeping around her,
you'd make yourself interrupt her, to mop
behind your sweeping. And Pequita—I saw her wrap
you up on the sofa when you had flu, and bring you
orange juice, as they'd taught her in school, for she
loved you, she was the person who loved you—
I saw too, that of what I wanted the university
to be for me—a tiny model of the city
with its own rules and subsets: "Tell me
each day who I am"—you'd found your part
in Pequita; I followed the shape
of your day touching center as it funneled
into her hand and moving pencil-point.

VI

For everything seemed natural to Pequita:
the Credo, her photocopied choir music
piled beside the tidy *prie-dieu*,
our neighborhood of syringe-filled gutters, drug-stoops and pimps,
her school's turkey cutouts, metal detectors, backed-up toilets . . .
Our human wilderness, half-urban, half-surreal
to her was a matter-of-fact Eden, like the picturesque ruins
and laughably rococo grottoes imagined

by the *seicento* as the Golden Age.
—And I, I thought her whole world, it comes back—
touching, as if her child's paradisial will were there
for my affectionate recreation, like our still faithfully,
occasionally, typed-up and dispatched
protests from the Ramp Committee to the Mayor. Slight effects
of perspective, tiny human gestures
giving point to the city's vast, ironic beauty.

PART TWO

VII

At a moment when no one was thinking
about her, Pequita awoke. Perhaps
she enjoyed the solitude, Pilar asleep,
me asleep across the street. She got up
and stood on the cheap oval bathroom rug
before the sink. At seven the drills started,
deeper-toned than ever before (they woke me)—
and part of your ceiling fell in; a beam
splintered, plummeting straight to the oval rug—
The person screaming over the phone
was Pilar. I thought it must be really
all right, or she'd be crying not screaming,
but when I'd called 911 and run over, Pequita
was barely alive.

        Then the hospital corridors,
me trying to close my winter coat
(the buttons were off) on my nightgown, you
on a bench, staring straight ahead.
When they said Pequita was
"gone," you were utterly silent. I brought you
to my place (though our street was a tangle
of police lights and yellow tape), terrified
of your fixed inner focus, as if you had
a plan . . . Next night I had Luz stay over,
I slept at her place; the third I was back. You,
thank God (I thought), were crying, and Luz

had set up the service. She propelled us downstairs
and to a tiny brick church I must often have passed
without seeing it, two blocks inland.

Egg-blue inside, it was, with a little green
and gilt altar, dark Stations on the walls,
and the statue of the Virgin of Guadeloupe
placed oddly below the altar stairs, so that Pilar,
after the death-mass, could kneel
before her, praying straight into her face,
while I on a kneeler buried mine in my hands.
What would the mother live for now, the hotel, me, or Luz,
already writing more endless mad letters? Yet only these
had from the City real answers: they'd brace the drill site
with vibration-absorbing piers; and they wanted
her and her friend Mrs. Citrin to know
"that no one else had been more than lightly injured."

VIII

It was the end of winter, very dark. The building
managers, nervy, had moved you to the first floor
next door, till you found a new place (I knew
you weren't looking). Each day I saw you
arrive from work, answer my call tersely,
then pull down your blinds. A shadow showed rarely,
flattened, shapeless; you lay on your sofa a lot.
"Thanks Anne—I'm better without company," or
"please understand." But often, later
in the evening, you'd come down the stairs
and turn inland. Then, one morning as I was passing
with early groceries, you were leaving the parish hall
in your black winter coat, heavily scarved,
and we paused. Approvingly, you tapped one glove
on my armload—you'd told me to cook more, dictated
recipes. I asked if this had been Pequita's
choir-practice place; the sentence wavered,
but you replied with grim joy,
"She's not practicing *now*." It took me a minute.
Pequita was singing, this moment, in the Presence.

Still what you felt most (it was in your face)
was absence, absence, but from something bitter
in your eyes, that seemed small and round with the cold, I felt
your desire to exclude me and our old collusive ironies.
What were such luxuries now, ironies, Anglo friends;
and I thought you hated my mind
that remembered the brownpapered books,
the orange juice. I reached to touch your arm—to get past
this, but no, you had to get home:
"I fasted for communion"; and your eyes

swerved away. All my laughable,
my lovely, delusional studies, that I'd seen you
sort through for Pequita, were now an affront. And yet
I felt you moving behind your own mind, as if
with something held in reserve . . .

IX

But then you stopped answering the phone, went
less often to church. What I thought
was that you were angry (certainly I was). Perhaps
I thought you needed to talk, and I'd visit you
in Manhattan. So one morning in March,
in the black coat I'd got for the funeral, I walked east
from the forty-second street Lexington stop
to the three-story, fairy-lit jungle atrium
of the Tricontinental, and went to the seventh floor,
where you started. There was a cart in the hall,

a gleaming chrome maid's cart half-projecting
from a bedroom. On its sides were rows
of glasses with lace sani-bonnets, gold-
stamped mini-soaps and deodorants. It moved out,
and you stood in the door with a sheet-load, looking fat
in a starchy pink uniform monogrammed
PILAR. When you saw me, you dropped the sheets
and in pain, pressed both palms to your cheeks,
and looked at me looking at you. When
I started sobbing, you took my shoulder and backed me
to the elevator. Pressed the button, stepped back,
and then, to my surprise, gave me a sudden hug
before pushing me in.

X

It had been always this half-connected
and tenuous, our friendship. What light on my own
isolation and need, that I hadn't known.
But you actually called me, that week, to propose
our old joke, a bridge walk—maybe Saturday?
Your voice in my ears sounded wobbly
with tension, held-backness, so I got in first:
a friend had wound up her doctorate and left me
a minute Village studio starting June . . . After that
I could listen, somber, as you poured out
your need to leave, Luz's cousin, the possible
hotel job "right in LA." You added "Anne," and broke off.
"Well, I'll tell you that later. Look, it may
snow on Saturday, OK?" "I don't care." And before

you hung up, I'd resigned you,
given you up. We'd part, on my side
in anger, on yours in oblivion. I met you
at the foot of the anchorage stair
(not the eastern approach, with its easy grade
near the ramp site). We climbed through the snow,
slowly, pausing at landings for different
views of our old alley world. Like a museum
of disused urban functions—we noted a bricked-over
backyard privy arch, and from higher, roof-huts, inkily distinct,
of old-style tenement dumbwaiters. The whole scene
thrown out of drawing by one of those giant
NYC cable-spools, charred at the bottom
where some homeless had tried to burn it.

The moist snow was sweeping
through the cable tower when we clambered
onto the path beneath it. As we moved, hunched slightly,
onto the mainspan, the whole city abruptly
whited-out to a monochrome geometry
of vertical and stooping gray lines. I thought
how Pequita would have loved it, and caught
her mother's eye. We went on cautiously, soon
pausing to stamp our boots and look over the rail
at the traffic lanes below us. "Anne, what
I started to say before—this is it: I'm sorry
I didn't talk to you—you understand?" "Of course,"
I lied aimlessly. But you, glancing sideways,
"But I'm *really* sorry . . ." "No, really . . ." You shook
your head slightly, then took my arm. "Okay then—
what's this thing?" pointing a snowy boot
at a bolt as high as our knees, with a rusted-on octagonal
nut: "It's just a bolt." You tapped your glove on a strut—
"strut," I provided. And you said, pompously, in Luz' very
intonations (in what spirit had you
listened?)—"The tolerances just aren't *there*."

Then, feeling easier, we started naming everything—
spikes, spun-wire vertical cables: English,
Spanish, and then I heard you speak Quiché (words once
for vines, for split trunks
over gorges?) But everything on the bridge was
shabby, neglected-looking; and you said
soberly: "If anyone was supposed
to look after this bridge, he's forgot all about it."
We didn't link arms again, but started back, pausing
to throw a few loose snowballs
on the Manhattan traffic below us. We'd go

our separate ways—I'd go on delaying, skirting
around my burnt-out places; you'd go
where you could, forget what you could—
some Job-like relinquishment of inquiry
or thought; organisms tend to persist . . . When
we got down to the massive base
of the anchorage, we managed a hug
that took in our past, at least: one embrace
of two black winter coats in the snow.

Cold-Water Flats

Laudate sie, Signore mio, per sor' Aqua
la quella è molt' utile e umile e prezios' e casta.
— FRANCIS OF ASSISI

From landing to landing, black-stockinged, white threads in a knot,
one woman hits at *forte* the scale from diaphragm to larynx.
Italian saws the cold air like a peddler
throwing a dog-Latin curse
over one shoulder, one fierce note
through our building's vast, indefinite rumor . . .
—*Guagliu!* (her grandson) *Vien' a ccà, vien' a pranza!*
By the light of a dangling bulb, at their kitchen tables, the students
grind at history, mathematics, courtly love . . .
The zinc-lidded bathtubs in their kitchens swarm
with gravid, amber-bellied roaches.
Across the court, in a Met broadcast, Puccini
fails to make one chord of twenty cold-water flats.

Electricity: direct current. Water-closets
(unheated) at the ends of the hallways. Each May,
the grandson himself comes by with a white-papered can
for "The Bride of Saint Francis." I've seen
the grandfather sweep his cash register clean
for just such a can—for two plastic-corded *fratelli*. He it was

chewed me out when I coolly bought his "Ground Meat for Pets"
at ten cents a pound. Ever after I must submit
to the complex folds of his frown, his mute overweighing
of ground beef in shining carnets of waxed paper. And then
all summer he'll rise, one hand on his sidewalk chair,
black-enameled, back-tilted among
the men's chairs as I pass
and touch his welt-seamed cap
not to me but to her

to *Donna Povertà!* barely tokened
in my ephemeral Village-poverty. In winter
the fire of his vision banks. Our piled-up
windows taped, our range-burners burning,
seven stories shudder each night as the super's wife
anathematizes the plumbing. Below me, even deep
in winter, the just-audible trickle
of Minetta Creek, bricked over
a century ago. Snowfalls. In Minetta Lane, ochre columns
of smoke from the garbage cans. And in the walls, from taps
in the sink and the tub, cold water. Its tang
of stone and metal, icy
at faucet-mouth, numbed lips, unceasing arrival, the water

which later, I think, will seem to have been
most precious—being useful, humble, chaste.

II. THE FIRST VERSE

The Depot

Sparrows tapping your shutter louvres? snow owls
guano your eaves? Spring rainstorms sway
in your gutters; down-cellar a green pipe pearls

and roots find its fissures. Matter—outside us, out in *le Vrai*,
matter—un-does; *fatiscit;* a sort of eternal
breakdown and sloughage. Small wonder that Saturday

finds you botanizing some mast-high aisle
in the Depot. Fazed by stock-names and numbers, distinctions
like drip-forged and molly- and carborundum-steel,

or, in DIMENSIONAL LUMBER, the trunk chart. Its dotted lines
follow core cuts, mere spindles, out to the perimeter or "wane,"
a ring of two-by-twelves with moonrim bark ribbons.

Yet even sparrows must nest-mend with worldstuff torn
out of somewhere. The joinery-bits in the MASTER JOINER
blister-pack point to his fast parataxes—copulas, common-

alities, ship-lists, figures in carpets or slimmer
hex-keys in sets, the eternal angle (Egyptian)
of iron plane-handles tuned to the unheard rumor

that joins them. The same slits repaired once with tendon-
thread in bone needles, bronze pins, the earliest factory-fittings
or the long floating line of the bass-baritone

Leporello, his *catàlogo* of continents and couplings
ironizing, admiring, down to the final mel-
isma on DOES (you know the Don's doings)

voi . . . sapete, voi . . . sapete . . . quel
che FA-AHH, ah-ahh, ah-ahh . . . Ah vowel
that winds through the world like a wind or a dowel,

you make us a clean dream of matter. Electrons wheel
translucent in orbit, sealants in lucid spheres fall
to our refts and rifts, you grout tubs and re-seal

turved huts in the rainy Carpathians where the Baal
Shem Tov ("the world is a wedding") lingers, and back to our own vernal
mall. You float like a bird through the darkening hall

of the Depot, cooling the brows of nocturnal
plasterers trailing meanders of lime-white prints
under parking-lot lights, past crepuscular forklifts, feral

carhoods streaming the fractalized shadows of chain links
and sledges laden with wattles, with yellowy rolls of oiled paper
to seal up the windows of snowy Muscovy or Minsk.

Villanelle

Bone-ivory thins out to sparkling gauze,
and the helices spell out their last revisions:
cascades of microscopic cellular flaws.

Dark quadrants in the X-rays of my jaws
mark the retreating toothbed, new excisions,
the ivory thinned out to sparkling gauze.

The synovial sea that bathed my knees withdraws,
leaving bone nubs to clickings and collisions,
cascades of calcium, microscopic flaws.

What's worse, this age of ice-flares and failed thaws
that might clear nights for rare auroral visions,
instead blows through my sleep like cradle-gauze,

filled with nursery-rockers, pastel night-lights: straws
that wove about those years of small decisions
a screen against the tide of cellular flaws.

Why should the ova and the menses pause
for this bleak text of lapses and elisions:
bone-ivory thinning out to sparkling gauze,
cascades of tiny intracellular flaws.

A Sonnet Map of Manhattan

Wall and Pine: The Rain

Now the god of rainy August hangs his mask
among the city's spires and balustrades
and stone clocktowers half-effaced in clouds.
On Park the first reflecting pool dims
with a thousand smelted-silver circle-rims,
while west on Fifth a modiste scatters leaves
in fall vitrines, and felt-browed mannequins
resign the world with gestures of disdain.

Now in the Cloister's high parterres the rain
floods copper gutterings, boxwood, terraced urns
and mottoes. "The weather turns." Clamped to their pier,
the smiling Gaul, the murderer Clotaire,
and Isaiah, green-throned, water-cowled, exchange
their fine-lit ironies for rotes of pain.

Houston Street: A Wino

They'd set up on Houston Street for the filming
of *Moscow on the Hudson*, and in his apartment
my father made himself up for his one-minute
turn in the filmic epiphany, set in a basement diner.

At the counter, the Russian defector regrets his defection
to the Fallen City, when at once a wino appears (it's the Fourth)
with a sparkler, staggering dazed unshaven phantasm
of lost America; the hero begins to smile,

and—musing still on the street, the red-painted
cast-iron facades scrimmed with posters and boarded
windows of ancient retail—realizes his girl will return

—which seeing quite unexpectedly
in a uptown theater, I startled a hundred
by crying out "That's my father" in the darkness.

East Fifth Street:
A Poster for the Oresteia

Pasted bumpily on brick, life-sized. Inside,
in a former foundry's casting vault, my father in the role
of Agamemnon died. A thin-browed bronze mask skating
the bath-stair: "Know that in this House

an archaic anger worked: a child burnt down to soot-marks,
a king and king's son coursed down the years." He took
the subway home at two a.m. He told me "Anne, if you're empty
and show it, empty *inside*, you'll be invisible

to muggers . . ." I've found this true. The audience,
tiptoeing off through the streetlit litter,
sees across the street, in a blackened vitrine,

three hovering shapes. Rag-shrouded heads,
long-skirted army coats and boots; and beneath the rags,
the dewlaps and the smirched muzzles of the Furies.

Greenwich Street: Sad Father with a Hat

Greenwich Street, sad father with a hat,
your smoked apartment shot with light-shaft light;
on weekend evenings, curled on your knee
as you read aloud, I could hear the tension flattening

your voice. Then lights-out, then the studied
half hour; and you'd slip through our tiny courtyard
into the late forties Village *noir,* its post-war notes
of lit-up streetlamps, of hatbrimmed shadows

gliding on brownstones and highwalled streets.
You were drifting westward towards the wharf-bars
past alleys where hatted shadows, featureless as felt,

embraced. And at breakfast, your arrowy cheekbones
blue-bruised, bruised by the men in blue
beneath whose knees, all night, you'd knelt.

MacDougal Street: Old-Law Tenements

We're aware in every nerve end of our tenement's
hand-mortared Jersey brick, the plumbing's
dripping dew-points, the electric running Direct,
and on each landing four hall-johns fitted

to the specifics and minima of the 1879
Tenement Housing Act. We live in its clauses
and parentheses, that drew up steep stairways
and filled the brown airwells with eyebrowed

windows. Unwhistling, the midwinter radiator
lists in its pool of rust. A lightcord winds
through its light chain; from a plasterless ceiling-slat

topples a roach, with its shadow. Downstairs, our Sicilian widow
beats the cold ribs with a long-handled skillet,
and faucets drum in twenty old-law flats.

East Eleventh Street: Three Images

A tenement door, a door set on its hinge
in the nineties, sheathed with brown-painted iron and dented
by the brooms of nocturnal rage . . . You must have lain
almost hugging it, the way our break-in rolled you

onto your back, left arm flung out. Two: unforgettable
inner-arm map of rucked veins, black punctures
and your fingers still slightly curled on the floor beneath
the dangling receiver. You managed to reach me, Ellen,

but no one could have reached you. No one wanted to reach you.
Only the friend too remote to hang up; then, three,
and all I'll keep of the whole thing, I swear it—the pre-dawn

bus ride across the city to your place, the strange
fawn light falling everywhere, on empty corners and diners,
the first coins dropping in the driver's metal bowl.

Eighteenth Street: The Brown Owl of Ulm

In a shuttered print shop, in silk-tied Morocco boards,
the staring oak owl of Ulm. It takes me from my browsing
back to the bombed-out, rebuilt cathedral, where I lifted,
one by one, the under-seat carvings of the "miraculously

untouched" Gothic choir seats. But someone has slipped
an old *Times* piece in here, about a photograph
that turned up after the War. Snapped in Ulm "at the time
of the transports"; perhaps from a confessional—

In the clear-obscure of the nave, three down-
tilted SS caps pore over columns of names.
Past the transept, glimpsed through a herd of coats,

bulging suitcases, lowered heads—past the altar—
a man with a child in his left arm stoops,
and with his right hand turns the carved eyes down.

First Avenue: Drive-In Teller

It's one half hour till Bank Wednesday—last day
for my monthly payment paid, though not in a car,
in the line of this East Side drive-in with its three-foot
mini-park, emerald shadows of ivy, pinks

in a six-inch border under dwarf juniper—
why mini-park for humble drive-in teller?
Now, in its capsule, my money rises vacuum-drawn,
noiseless through transparent tubes, and vanishes

into glossy carport ceiling, then bobs and plummets
with aviatic speed to Oriental cashier, beautiful as princess
Turandot by moonlight, in her silicon cell which monitors

three lanes. Each surveyed by a gray security
lens, angled towards license plates, which puts on film
unseen by human eyes, our strange transaction . . .

Sixty-seventh Street: Tosca *with Man in Bedrock*

The Met's first winter broadcast. Tosca, rimmed
by the clouded silk of her gown, lets fall
one by one the pure drops of the *Vissi d'arte*,
and the cantilevered mezzanine, underlit,

stipple-eyed in its stoles and fur tippets, hangs
breathless. Straight down, past sallow platforms, sewer
outfalls and steam lines, the man in the bedrock
side-steps in his worklamp's flattened yellow,

spools out more wire, lowers his radio probe
to the back of a sunken centenary main
(fed by watersheds in the still half-glacial Catskills)

and hears, through bell curves of *pings*, each note
vibrate off his shaft of Precambrian schist. Gray, void . . .
our Manhattan Schist, laid down too early for fossils.

100 Riverside: Waking Up at Mari's

The city through her back-bedroom window: a shift-
ing of trash cans (snow-crunch of galvanized steel), gear
sounds drowned in metal hulls, horns now: one by one to lift,
fine-tune, and weigh my home town: *here, here!*

I let go, as passivest listeners listen, to sift
the city, naming sounds, for named sounds near
or distant make a depth where my too deft
attention—deep and troubled, city too endeared—

can lose itself. Always to arrive, and hear
on such first wakings everything that lives
within me sigh, as if to say *all's well, all's here,*

as if the old rifts in this reft
being were annealed. —AS IF is what it is. It's theft
of all that is. And nothing else is dear.

One-forty-sixth Street: My Stepmother's Chloral

The last months before you drank it,
endless nights of your violence driving me out
to the street . . . It would start at dinner. Your chalky,
opaque skin, your orange-dun freckles and brows—I knew

every hair, every shade of the obsessions that shifted and sat
inside you, looking out, the me-hatred whose outward
vector kept you, awhile, alive . . . You were putting
the final touches on all of us—on me, as I fled

down the stairs to the stoop; what face did I find?
—the city's exquisite indifference drew me.
Curb-balancing on my sneaker arches, still and late
on Broadway, then strolling south for hours . . . I was fourteen,
and then I was fifteen—you drank the chloral and

                                   I was free!

I lived my factitious joy as you lived your factitious hate.

One-sixty-fifth Street: The Currency Exchange

Here money takes on more palpable form, moist bills and coins
counted out on linoleum sills. It's July on Broadway,
and the Exchange is a 12' by 12' storefront
whose transom sports one outspread, sooted handprint.

FOR YOUR CONVENIENCE AND SAFETY
YOUR TRANSACTION WILL BE PHOTOGRAPHED
by a bullet-headed, cyclopean rod.
Before me, under gray ponytail, a black vinyl jacket's

hand-painted with bull in cave-art outline, pizzle trailing
three hairs to the ground. Most here, bankless, bear
welfare checks or payroll, from which the Exchange

takes its meek percentage. Others, like me, hold warning-red
envelopes for phone bills, electric; for these are those who pay,
always, on the final, disconnection, day.

One-sixty-eighth Street: The Armory

As the mast-riggings atop the Empire State flare
to the trembling of air-engines, as the massive
apartment towers of Central Park West
lie flat in the cold green of the lake . . .

As the ears of Pan Am's landing pads grow tense
when helicopters drop like handkerchiefs from the evening,
and the subwayman walking his check-walk, grid-lit
from above, bows his head from spike to spike, and tie to tie . . .

the island battens for winter. Through a window crack, icy air
freshens the Armory's vault-room, where seas
of snowy cots sleep tenement families

when Con Ed cuts off their defaulted tenements;
since from under old piles of boxed-up battle gear
the city's gas mains still bring gas heat here.

One-seventy-fifth Street: The Scout

No one is present. The money's metamorphosed, moving
in electrons on a copper strip. It's no time, or one;
unseen, the money crosses the dateline where the bulk
of the earth still lies in shadow, following the line

until it condenses like vapor on hardscrabble farms
slashed from the jungle; soon essence of poppy will flow
where nothing else and no one will willingly go . . .
The beeper. Phone booths by the spike-fenced junior high

in a neighborhood whose sewer is crumbling, where last week
tuberculosis was diagnosed; the money flows
from the bridge to the streets below. Our stoopfronts sprout

silhouettes with baseball caps—the signifying angles, colors, the
passwords. And on the stoop front, the watching profile
and elliptic, archaic, smile of the ten-year-old scout.

The First Verse

Breshit bara elohim et ha-shamayim v-et ha-eretz.
— GENESIS 1:1

I
My black-lettered Hebrew Bible, dense
and doughty as a cobble. The Bible in Hebrew—irreducible!
Yet at the first verse, a hair-thin net of cracks
appears, each crack a vast highway, and wildly we leap
onto this first, this universal, cobble, *BRESHIT*. "In-the-beginning."
Or maybe, "In-the-beginning-of." Of what, you may ask—of "making"?
 Maybe—
and so the slight break ramifies and blooms
into shelf-feet of commentaries, monographs, and now
you must swiftly ransack your Sumerian—
yes, without Enuma Elish there's no understanding the matter—
For it seems that that stately cosmogony begins
with just such another hermetic, mind-boggling ellipsis;
and so the two master-texts, with archaic courtesy, nod
across the millennia. But I forgot to mention
the Crimean War. It seems the war upset the local
Karaites, who saddled up and fled
to St. Petersburg, taking their cherished, oldest dated
scrolls of the Bible, wrapped, for freshness, in date leaves, and left them

in the public library. But naturally, the public library!
And so these sectarians, not even actually, exactly,
Jewish—the rabbis' deep-dyed foes—preserved the inerrant Word,
though not without hosts of tiny scribal errors
some day to set shuddering
whole forests of editors, compositors, microfilmers—

II

BARA. Verb, transitive, sacred, used with no Subject but
God, translation "made." We'll do well to pause
for the comment of Rashi, winding forth
from the medieval balconies of Troyes:
"The world is made for Torah." For this very sentence!
(The lovely sentence—the terrible world.) A floating circule
above BARA reminds us to look below
our Biblical text with its verse-carets, vowel-points and the jots
that flourish the great text with the summery human voice,
for the medieval mine of the Masora,
coded word-frequencies (frequently upbraiding Bible)
with its own typeface, learned circles, note-makers, exception-takers—
How world upon subworld attests the young Creator
riding the stormwind with earth and moon in his hands,

III

ELOHIM. The third word in the Bible is
"God." Well, literally, "gods," but by convention—
except in pagan contexts—though Christians, too,
find Trinity adumbrations here, faint rushes
of the Presence-packed Unseen. Yet our verb
is a singular verb; God alone is God; and anyway, BARA
is male. —What next, a verb should be male? Yes. For such
is the nature of that mode of being
which is the Bible. God, whether singular
or in himself the very host of Heaven,
is male.—But what about goddess Tiamat? Did you know that in Enuma Elish

her wrestling with god conceives our world? Her very name
is cognate to the "deep" (*tehom*) God moves on. Though of course
the Enuma Elish is *not* the Bible. And isn't there something
columnar and stark, and, well, male
about this first verse? (Though this goddess sprouts up
in the Psalms, as well . . .)

IV

ET. . . ET? The fourth word in the Bible,
ET? Yes, and the sixth. Translation: asterisk. Even in Hebrew-
English Interlinear, darkly forbidden to students,
asterisk. (The Lexicon adds *Mark of the accus.*)
In fact, this recurrent biblical
—unword, reflects the perception
that verbs, in accusing their nouns, comb them out
from the static of the Indeterminate. Think of the Karaites,
how amidst the grapeshot, the dusty saddlery
and willow baskets, they bore off their Bible. And there it lay,
now the Leningrad Codex (L), until the Stuttgart professor
pored deeply upon it, and then Kittel proceeded
to make his historic redaction. How leisurely his world
seems from our chaos, a single late-twenties afternoon
of peaceful scholarship . . . His fanatical accuracy, the fonts
made to his specifications, his beautifully intelligible
face, melted down in the carpet-bombing of Leipzig—

V

HA-SHAMAYIM. The heavens. This word
reminds you of Arabic *sham*, as Allah recalls *EL*
or *ELOHIM*, God. Not to mention God's own
self name, the Tetragrammaton, supreme
and half-conjugate IS. Shielded, irradiant core of being, never right-printed
    or uttered
(in English suppressed, in Hebrew mis-voweled), so that
we students, reciting aloud, approaching again and again the great letters

must stammer out LORD or else NAME . . .
For so the word is still set up in our time. Even Kittel,
meticulous scholar and (I've never seen this in print), root-and-branch
anti-Semite, whose very professorship, it is whispered . . . But wait. Isn't
    this our own
Biblia Hebraica, Kittel's BHK? No. Look. This is now "Hebrew Bible
of Stuttgart" (BHS)—new preface, Masora, even from Leningrad
microfilms, new—the K is no more. And why not? You know
why not. Every try to look up
Endlösung, Final Solution, in a modern German-
English Dictionary? Well, it's not there. And where
a word isn't, mightn't *anything* be? You could replace *BRESHIT*
with "In the beginning the Word"—and *voilà*, you're in Chartres. Why not?
On the right, Jesse's stem, overhead
Heaven's Queen in her rose—is this too the Bible? North of the transept
the cult-statue stands, Black Virgin of Chartres,
her apron lost in initialed bronze tablets,

toes curling, planted on her ancient pillar
which lips of brides caress for centuries,
while tourists stream in before the majesty of *EL* . . .

VI

V—Hebrew character *vav*—is for "and." Then *ET* returns, the sixth word, the
    Un-word. As when
on the threshing-floor of Nachon, the abstracted Uzzah
put his hand forth to steady the holy ark
of the LORD, for the oxen shook it. But God
kindled against him; he died; so that David, fearing, refused
to take the ark of the LORD into the city.

VII

Seventh word, last word. HA-ERETZ, the earth. Can it really,
this temple-built, mosque-planted, stave-churched and belfry'd earth,
be made for Torah? For Rashi is still,
as medieval people loved to do, explaining the Bible. His argument, crotchety
and scholastic as Romanesque
capitals where one biblical name, Tubal-Cain, for example, takes on
a florid history, five wives, and murders with a cross-bow;
and the Virgin goes on nursing among the heiratic, sympathizing
beasts' faces, angular as those Old Hebrew
characters like fishhooks and little horns

(for the Biblical characters before us not *exactly*
Hebrew—Chaldean. Aramaic.) Yet everything's here. As in the delicate
midrash where Moses stands weeping
because he is copying down the words
describing his own death, hither-side of Jordan. The lovely
sentence, the terrible world—the beginning. Inerrant,
perfect, the first seven words of the Bible.